387.7

W9-AOM-194

TO SPACE AND BACK
The Story of the Shuttle

BY
SUSAN DUDLEY GOLD

CRESTWOOD
HOUSE

New York

Maxwell Macmillan Canada
Toronto

Maxwell Macmillan International
New York Oxford Singapore Sydney

Library of Congress Cataloging-in-Publication Data
Gold, Susan Dudley.
    To space and back: the story of the shuttle/by Susan Dudley Gold. —1st ed.
        p. cm. — (Adventures in space)
    Includes bibliographical references and index.
    Summary: Examines the history, uses, and accomplishments of the space shuttle program.
ISBN 0-89686-688-2
    1. Space shuttles—Juvenile literature. 2. Space flight—Juvenile literature. 3. Challenger (Spacecraft)—
Juvenile literature. [1. Space shuttles. 2. Space flight. 3. Outer space—Exploration.]
I. Title. II. Series: Space (Series)
TL795.5.G67 1992   629.44'1—dc20   91-42565

Photo Credits
All photos/illustrations courtesy of the National Aeronautics and Space Administration (NASA).

Design
Tina Tarr-Emmons

Layout and Production
Custom Communications

Copyright © 1992 by Crestwood House, Macmillan Publishing Company

Macmillan Publishing Company
866 Third Avenue
New York, NY 10022

**CRESTWOOD
HOUSE**

Maxwell Macmillan Canada, Inc.
1200 Eglinton Avenue East
Suite 200
Don Mills, Ontario M3C 3N1

First edition
Printed in the United States of America
10 9 8 7 6 5 4 3 2 1

Macmillan Publishing Company is part of the Maxwell
Communication Group of Companies.

CONTENTS

"WE DELIVER"

O n November 11, 1982, the world's highest flying "moving van" blasted off with its cargo for space. The moving van was the space shuttle *Columbia*, on its first real mission. Aboard were two satellites owned by Satellite Business Systems and Telesat of Canada. The two companies had hired the **shuttle** to carry their **satellites** into space. Satellites are small bodies that **orbit**, or circle, larger bodies in space.

On the day of the launch, the spacecraft lifted off without a minute's delay. Piloting the craft was the **astronaut** Robert F. Overmyer. Commander Vance D. Brand was in charge of the flight. Dr. Joseph P. Allen and Dr. William B. Lenoir were also on board. It was up to them to release the satellites. It was the first time the shuttle had carried cargo to be delivered to space.

Space shuttle Discovery *lifts off Launchpad 39A at the Kennedy Space Center on January 22, 1992. Inset: The crew of* Columbia *in 1982 on the first shuttle mission after four test flights: Commander Vance Brand (holding sign); (clockwise) William Lenoir, Robert Overmyer and Joseph Allen.*

Columbia's engines guided the spacecraft into orbit around Earth. The shuttle's cargo bay, in the back section, held the satellites. At just the right moment, Dr. Lenoir and Dr. Allen released the locks holding the satellites and sent them into space.

Forty-five minutes later, rockets on each satellite fired. This sent them into higher orbits, where they stayed circling over the same spot on Earth. By bouncing messages off the satellites, people on opposite sides of Earth could talk to each other. The space delivery was a success.

The proud shuttle crew held up a sign for the world to see on TV. It read THE ACE MOVING CO. FAST AND COURTEOUS SERVICE. WE DELIVER.

A REUSABLE SPACESHIP

Columbia is a new kind of spaceship. Like the Apollo missions that took Americans to the Moon and back, the shuttle takes off like a rocket. Once in space it flies like a spacecraft. But returning to Earth, the shuttle does not parachute into the ocean as other U.S. spaceships did. Instead it puts down landing gear and glides to the ground like an airplane. Then, after a checkup and a few repairs, it is ready for another flight.

The first test flight of the space shuttle *Columbia* took off from the Kennedy Space Center in Florida on April 12, 1981, with the astronauts John W. Young and Robert L. Crippen aboard. It returned to Earth two days later.

Other spaceships are used only once. The shuttle is

designed for at least 100 flights. Its goal is to provide cheap rides to space for people and cargo. It is called a shuttle because it makes trips back and forth like a shuttle bus. But its route runs through space instead of city streets.

In the 1960s and 1970s Americans watched in awe as astronauts flew into space. On their TVs viewers watched men walk on the Moon and return to Earth. The early space program's flights proved that people could survive in space. But the flights cost a lot of money. Each spacecraft cost millions of dollars to build and could be used only once. Each needed a giant rocket to lift off from Earth.

In 1969, three months before the first man set foot on the Moon, the **National Aeronautics and Space Administration (NASA)** formed the Space Shuttle Task Group. NASA is the agency that runs the U.S. space program. By September the group had proposed forming a new space transportation system (STS). It would feature a reusable shuttle to carry people and cargo to space.

In 1972 President Richard M. Nixon gave NASA the go-ahead to build the shuttle. He and the U.S. Congress saw the shuttle program as a good deal. It promised to make space flight cheaper and easier. NASA chose Rockwell International to build the first shuttles.

NASA had great plans for the space shuttle. It would orbit Earth for seven days, then be ready for another flight 14 days later. By 1986 the agency planned to have a fleet of four shuttles making 12 to 15 flights a year.

Private companies would pay NASA to carry cargo into space. NASA planned to build large power plants in space to provide solar energy for Earth. The shuttle would also transport workers and materials for a space station to be built in space.

Two solid rocket boosters, along with three main engines, provide the thrust to carry space shuttle Discovery into space on January 22, 1992. It was Discovery's 15th mission and the 45th of the shuttle program.

The space station, planned to be finished by the year 2000, would serve as a permanent space lab. It might also someday serve as a base for flights to Mars.

The shuttles were named after sailing ships used in scientific research or exploration. *Columbia*, the first shuttle, is named after a small sailing ship that explored the Columbia River. *Columbia* is also the name of one of the first U.S. Navy ships to travel around the world. The crew of America's first Moon mission also chose *Columbia* as the name of their spaceship.

The name of the second shuttle, ***Challenger***, came from a U.S. Navy research ship that sailed in the 1870s. Its first launch was on April 4, 1983.

Discovery, first launched on August 30, 1984, was named for two sailing ships. The first, Henry Hudson's ship, searched for the Northwest Passage between the Atlantic and Pacific oceans in the 1600s. The second, captained by James Cook, discovered Hawaii in the 1700s.

The fourth shuttle built, *Atlantis*, got its name from a two-masted sailing ship used for research from 1930 to 1966. *Atlantis* was first launched on October 3, 1985.

The newest shuttle, *Endeavour*, was named by school-children in a NASA contest. The winning name is from another of Captain Cook's ships, which explored the South Seas in 1768. *Endeavour* was launched for the first time on May 7, 1992, with a crew of seven.

The tiles on the shuttle's body gleam white like the sails on those earlier exploring ships. Its passengers are astronauts, whose name comes from Greek words meaning "star sailors."

The first shuttle missions were numbered one through nine. In 1984 NASA changed the number system. Each mission had two numbers and a letter. The first number stood for the fiscal year in which the flight was planned. The second number was for its landing site (one for the Kennedy Space Center, two for the Vandenberg Air Force Base). The letter showed the order in which the flights were scheduled.

Mission 41-B of the *Challenger* was planned for 1984, landed at the Kennedy Space Center and was second on the schedule.

Today shuttle missions are once again numbered by the old system. The November 1991 flight of *Atlantis* was numbered STS-44. It marked the 44th flight of the space transportation system.

THE SHUTTLE INSIDE AND OUT
Orbiter

T he main body of the shuttle is the **orbiter**. It is about the size of a DC-9 jet. It is made of aluminum and is 122 feet long and 57 feet high. Its wings measure 78 feet.

Almost 30,000 silicon tiles cover 70 percent of the orbiter. They protect it from heat when it takes off and lands. The tiles have led some to nickname the shuttle the flying brickyard. The tiles can stand heat up to 2,300° F and can be red-hot on one side and cool on the other. They are expected to last 100 flights, though some are replaced every mission.

The shuttle's three main engines are in the rear of the orbiter. Also in the rear are two smaller engines that power the shuttle into and out of orbit.

Astronauts aboard Endeavour, NASA's newest shuttle orbiter, hold a wayward satellite in place until it can be brought into the shuttle's cargo bay. The satellite, Intelsat VI, was later fitted with a booster and released into space.

Flight Deck

Inside the orbiter is a cabin with two levels. On the upper level is the **flight deck** where the shuttle is run. Below is the **mid-deck** where the crew lives and works.

There are three types of crew members on board the shuttle. The **commander** and **pilot**, chosen by NASA, run the shuttle. The commander is in charge of the spacecraft, the crew and the success of the mission. It is up to the commander to keep the mission safe.

The pilot is second in command and helps the commander. He or she may help operate the **robot arm** to load or unload a satellite or other cargo.

A second type of crew member is the **mission specialist**. Two to three mission specialists fly on most missions. They too are astronauts chosen and trained by NASA. Their duties are to plan all activities on the shuttle and keep things running smoothly. They are in charge of the equipment needed for payloads and experiments. Many are scientists.

Mission specialists must know a lot about space shuttle systems. They are experts on using the robot arm and other equipment. For some missions they need to know how to walk and work in space. During lift-off and landing, they control the payload to make sure it does not harm the shuttle.

The third type of crew member is the **payload specialist**. Usually one to four payload specialists fly aboard each flight. They are in charge of the payload. The company that owns the payload chooses the payload specialists, but they must be approved by NASA. Payload specialists are not career astronauts. One of their jobs is to repair and start up satellites in space.

The pilot and commander sit at the controls at the front of the flight deck. The shuttle can be piloted from either seat. Four identical computers control the shuttle. They all run at once, checking each other hundreds of times a second. Three of the four computers must agree before an order is carried out. A fifth computer is kept running as a spare in case one of the others breaks down.

Each computer is contained in two 55-pound boxes about the size of small suitcases. Machines attached to the cases feed the computer information about the shuttle's flight. Other machines follow the computers' orders to steer the shuttle. The shuttle can also be steered by hand. Under normal conditions the only controls the pilot has to run are the landing gear and the brakes during landing.

The control panel has more than 2,020 switches, dials and displays. To make the shuttle as safe as possible, each important system has three controls. If one or two fail a third takes over. The shuttle has more than three times the number of controls the Apollo spacecraft had. It has 100 times more controls than a car dashboard has.

Four people can ride on the flight deck. A mission specialist sits behind the pilot to the right. There he or she oversees the operations inside the shuttle and the experiments being conducted on board. To the left is a payload specialist, who controls switches that open and close the **payload bay** door where the cargo is stored.

Other switches run the robot arm, the lights and the TV

in the payload bay. The 50-foot robot arm has a shoulder, elbow and wrist that move. Its four-claw hand can grab a satellite and push it into space or bring it back for repairs. A TV camera on the robot arm's wrist shows what it is doing. It can also be used to look at the outside of the shuttle to check for problems.

Six triple-pane windows over the control panels offer a good view of space. Two more windows are overhead, and one is in the hatch. The cargo can be seen through two windows in the payload bay.

The air inside the cabin is about the same as on Earth, a mix of oxygen and nitrogen. Inside temperatures range from 61° F to 85° F. A filter keeps the air cleaner than on Earth. It removes pollution, pollen and odor.

There is no **gravity** in space. Gravity is the force that pulls us toward the Earth. Without it people float, and their bodies feel as if they weigh nothing. Special gear in the cabin helps the crew cope with the effects of no gravity. Seat belts hold crew members in their seats. Tables and desks are clamped to the walls. The astronauts even have suction cups on the bottoms of their shoes to stay in one place.

Mid-deck

The crew's home is in the bottom level, or mid-deck, of the cabin. Compared to the cramped Apollo spaceships, the shuttle's cabin is fairly roomy. The mid-deck is 13 feet by 12 feet by 9 feet. Much of the space along the walls is filled with gear.

Astronaut Daniel C. Brandenstein (left) sits in the pilot's seat in a mock-up of a shuttle flight deck at the Johnson Space Center. Mission specialist Guion S. Bluford, Jr., (right) occupies a seat behind the pilot. The two astronauts were practicing for their flight aboard the Challenger *in August 1983.*

From the flight deck, crew members enter the mid-deck through a 26-by-28-inch hatch. As they enter, the toilet, basin and kitchen area are to the left. To the right are the crew's bunks and lockers. Straight ahead a wall of lockers stores food and other supplies. To the rear a sealed passage leads to the payload bay and outside.

The passage, or **air lock**, is a 63-by-83-inch drum. There astronauts change into space suits before entering the payload bay or going into space. The sealed air lock keeps the cabin's air and pressure from escaping when the outside hatch is open.

Floor panels under the mid-deck can be lifted to store trash and supplies.

Payload Bay

The shuttle's cargo, or **payload**, is kept in a large space, called a bay, to the rear of the cabin. The payload may be a satellite like that aboard *Columbia*. Or it may be a spacecraft to be launched from space. Other times the shuttle carries a space laboratory, called Spacelab, in the payload bay. The shuttle can carry payloads up to 65,000 pounds. Large doors in the bay can be opened to release the payload into space.

Astronaut Bruce McCandless tests the robot arm of the space shuttle Challenger *during* a mission in February 1984.

COMPLEX FLYING MACHINE

N *ewsweek* magazine has called the shuttle "the most complex flying machine ever built." It combines the features of planes, spacecraft and gliders. It uses both solid fuel and liquid hydrogen to soar into space.

Three main engines, fueled by liquid hydrogen, and two **solid rocket boosters** launch the shuttle into space. At 6.6 seconds before lift-off, the main engines are started. Liquid hydrogen stored in a giant **external tank** attached to the orbiter powers the engines. The tank also contains liquid oxygen to make the hydrogen burn. The engines burn 64,000 gallons of fuel per minute. The power they produce could light New York City.

The solid rocket boosters are attached to the giant tank to the right and left of the orbiter. Each solid rocket booster contains fuel, **oxidizer** to make the fuel burn and an ignition motor. The ignition flame reaches 5,250° F to start the booster's fuel burning. In less than half a second the booster is burning at full steam.

As the fuel burns it produces hot gases. The gases are forced through the nozzle in the center of the booster. This creates a great deal of pressure. The force of the gases leaving the nozzle pushes the booster forward. This forward push is called **thrust**. Each booster produces more than one million pounds of thrust. Once ignited, the boosters cannot be turned off. Some people call them controlled bombs because of this.

Discovery waits for lift-off on Launchpad 39A at the Kennedy Space Center in Florida. The space shuttle's solid rocket boosters can be seen on either side of the orbiter. The external tank between the solid rocket boosters is the largest part of the shuttle.

Space shuttle Columbia *touches down on the dry lake bed at Edwards Air Force Base in California. Inset:* Space shuttle Endeavour *is transported on the back of NASA's new shuttle carrier aircraft. After a brief stopover at the Johnson Space Center in Houston, Texas (in the background), the new shuttle will fly to the Kennedy Space Center in Florida.*

The force of the boosters and the main engines lifts the shuttle, its crew and its cargo into space. The astronauts feel as if they are riding on a fast carnival ride. Then they soar into space and weightlessness.

The solid rocket boosters burn up in two minutes. Their casings drop off and fall into the ocean, where they are retrieved. They are cleaned and inspected, then refilled with fuel and reused.

As the shuttle nears orbit at about 70 miles high, the engines shut off. Ten to 15 seconds later, the large fuel tank drops away from the shuttle and lands in the Indian Ocean. Most of it burns up as it speeds through the air. It is one of the few parts of the shuttle that is not reused.

A computer on the engines starts them and shuts them off. It also checks the amount of oxygen and hydrogen being fed to the engines. Fifty times a second the computer checks the engines' temperature, pressure and speed.

Once in space the shuttle's two smaller engines fire. These engines force the shuttle into orbit around Earth. Traveling at 17,500 mph, the shuttle circles Earth every 90 minutes.

When the mission is completed, the shuttle's two rear engines slow its speed, and it drops out of orbit and moves toward Earth. The air slows the shuttle as it nears Earth. It heads toward runways in Florida or California that are almost three miles long, much longer than those at a regular airport.

A microwave landing system guides the shuttle to the right spot on the runway. The pilot lowers the landing gear and applies the brakes after the shuttle touches the ground. The shuttle lands like a glider. The landing must be perfect, because the shuttle cannot circle the runway and try again. It lands while traveling at more than 200 mph. A parachute attached to the newest shuttle, *Endeavour*, will slow it down during landing. The parachute system is also being installed in the older shuttles.

After landing, the orbiter is flown back to the Kennedy Space Center on the back of a 747 jet. Workers there get it ready for the next flight.

PREPARING FOR FLIGHT

D uring the early days of the space program, astronauts had to be jet pilots and no older than 35. Because the cabins were so small, they had to be shorter than 5 feet 11 inches. They became experts on the stars, space, rockets and computers and took hundreds of tests. It took them several years to get ready for space flight.

The shuttle allows more people to enter space. No longer does each space traveler have to be a jet pilot. Scientists and other experts have jobs on the shuttle too. Each crew member is an expert on one part of the space mission.

Spacecraft have bigger cabins now, so astronauts no longer have to be below a certain height. New technology has made it easier to eat and live in space. People in good health can make the trip without much trouble. Each shuttle flies with a crew of two to eight people. The trips now last a week or more.

Training

NASA astronauts—pilots, commanders and mission specialists—go through a one-year training course. To get into the course, pilots must have flown jets for at least 1,000 hours. The top pilots are chosen as commanders. Mission specialists must have worked in their fields for at least three years. Each must pass a medical exam and have a college degree. About 100 women and men are now training to be astronauts.

Like other crew members, payload specialists must pass health and fitness tests. They need 180 hours of training to learn about the payload. If the cargo is complex they may have to study even longer. They also learn how the shuttle operates and what to do in an emergency. Some payload specialists may start training two years before a mission.

Training for the crew members takes place at the Johnson Space Center in Texas. Machines and special tests record how crew members' bodies and minds will react when they are weightless. A **KC-135 jet**, nicknamed the vomit comet, is used for the tests. The jet flies in a special pattern that makes the crew weightless for up to 30 seconds. While floating they practice eating, drinking and using gear.

An underwater tank is used to copy the weightless feeling for a longer time. Inside the tank, crew members practice moving around while floating in water. Floating in water is similar to floating in space.

Astronauts Bruce McCandless and Joseph P. Kerwin, dressed in space suits, train for the weightlessness of space in an underwater tank at the Marshall Space Flight Center in Alabama.

Crew members also practice in a dummy shuttle called a **simulator**. It looks like the inside of the real shuttle, with a flight deck, a mid-deck and a payload bay. Even the view out the windows looks as it would in space. A computer trains the astronauts how to react if something goes wrong. For some the training seems so real they feel they have already flown in space by the session's end.

Ten weeks before lift-off, the simulator is linked to mission control. Mission control is the team at the Johnson Space Center that guides the shuttle while it is in space. During this time all crew members and the mission control team do their jobs as if it is a real flight.

The commander and pilot train for 600 hours in the simulator. They also practice landing KC-135 jets or Grumman Gulfstream II planes.

At least two crew members must be able to do the most important parts of each job. Then if someone becomes sick or hurt, the flight can continue.

Three days before the launch the crew moves to the Flight Crew Training Building at the Kennedy Space Center in Florida. All flights are launched from there.

When they return to Earth crew members go to the Johnson Space Center. There they spend several days telling NASA about the trip. Often they have tips to help make the flights easier for future crews. Then they answer reporters' questions. After a few days off they head back to the Johnson Space Center to train for another flight.

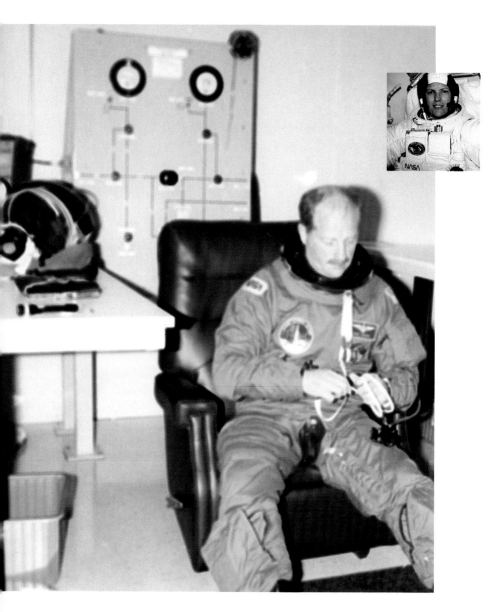

Mission commander Frederick H. Hauck straps himself into a pressure suit
in preparation for mission STS-26 aboard space shuttle Discovery. It was
the first shuttle flight after the Challenger exploded during lift-off on January
28, 1986. Inset: Mission specialist Kathryn D. Sullivan wears a space suit
minus the helmet aboard Discovery during mission STS-31 in April 1990.
The crew launched the Hubble space telescope during the flight.

Suiting Up

On early flights astronauts wore space suits for the entire trip. Now they wear more comfortable clothes during the flight. The cabin has its own oxygen and temperature controls, so no special clothing is needed.

Inside the spacecraft the astronauts wear knit shirts and slacks, lined zippered jackets and soft slippers. All the clothing has been treated so it is fireproof. Pockets with flaps that close keep the astronauts' personal items from floating away. The space travelers pack pens, pencils, sunglasses, notebooks, jackknives and scissors.

During lift-off and return to Earth, astronauts pull on special pressurized suits. These suits are also used if the air in the cabin becomes polluted or if the astronauts need to bail out. The suits are attached to parachutes in case of an emergency.

Astronauts wear complete space suits when working in space. These are stored in the air lock between the mid-deck and the payload bay. The suits protect the astronauts from heat and cold and provide oxygen to breathe.

In the 1960s and 1970s the Apollo astronauts wore space suits made just for them. Today's space suits are designed to last at least eight years and are made to be worn by different people. They come in three sizes and are worn by both men and women.

On board the shuttle, astronauts have a toilet. Outside

the cabin other methods have to be used. Astronauts wear plastic bags with tubes attached to collect the urine under their space suits. The urine is dumped into the waste system on board the shuttle when the astronauts return. Solid waste is stored in other bags.

Next to the skin each astronaut wears mesh underwear cooled by water tubes. The upper and lower parts of the space suit are put on like a shirt and pants. The space suit's pants go on first. The upper part is hard fiberglass and has a built-in life-support system. The astronaut floats up and into the upper part, which hangs from the wall in the air lock. Then he or she snaps the two sections together and seals them with special rings.

Each suit comes with a 21-ounce bag of water to drink. Instruments attached to the astronaut record the body's reactions for doctors back on Earth. A "Snoopy" cap contains headphones and microphones to keep in touch with others.

Last to go on are the gloves, visor and helmet. The visor and helmet protect the wearers from the Sun's harmful rays and from tiny meteors that speed through space.

The suits are easier to move in than the stiff outfits of the 1960s and 1970s. Bearings in the joints of the suits let astronauts bend, lean and twist. The largest space suit weighs 107 pounds.

Astronauts working outside the cabin carry tools in a small workstation attached to their suits. Lights on their helmets brighten the area while they work in the darkness of space. When Edward White first walked in space in 1965, he breathed through a 25-foot cord attached to the spaceship. Today built-in units and backpacks give astronauts more freedom. They no longer have to be hooked to the spaceship.

To get around in space, astronauts wear backpacks, called manned maneuvering units (MMUs). They are powered by gas. When the gas is released each astronaut moves in the opposite direction. The astronaut uses hand controls to move about. The unit has two power systems and weighs 310 pounds. If one power system fails, the second carries the astronaut back to safety.

Usually a shuttle has only two full space suits on board. In a crisis the other crew members can put on their launch and entry suits. If necessary the shuttle can return to Earth within an hour after leaving orbit.

Rest and Exercise

To keep in shape during a shuttle flight, astronauts follow an exercise plan. They walk on a treadmill locked to the floor of the cabin. Straps hook the astronauts to the treadmill. In their free time, they play cards and games, read or listen to taped music.

On the Apollo flights the crew members slept in hammocks or tied themselves to the wall. Today's astronauts sleep in bunk beds. Each bunk has a light, a fan and a two-way radio. Ties on the sheets keep the sleeping astronauts from floating around the cabin. Special blankets muffle sounds.

If there is no room for bunk beds on the flight the crew members sleep in sleeping bags. Tied to the crew's lockers, the sleeping bags float upright or out flat. Without gravity there is no up or down, so the crew can sleep in any position.

Chow Time

Planning a menu for a space crew is no easy matter. The food must provide nutrition and keep from spoiling on long flights. With little room for extras, food must be lightweight and not take up much space. The crew adds one more condition: It must *taste* good.

During the first space flights, the crew members squeezed their food from tubes. They had no trouble swallowing in space, but they did not ask for seconds. The food was pasty and tasteless.

Other crews tried eating bite-sized cubes of food. They had to chase the crumbs before they floated away. One crumb could ruin a mission if it got lodged in an important piece of equipment. Later the cubes of food were coated with gelatin to prevent crumbs.

Some foods were dried and packed in plastic. To eat, the astronauts cut off a corner of the bag and squirted water into the food. They could shoot hot or cold water from a squirt gun stored in the cabin. Wedged into a corner to keep from floating, the crew ate one item at a time.

On board the shuttle the meals are much more pleasant. There are many foods that can now be taken into space. Crew members eat together, each with his or her own tray. The trays join together to form a table. Instead of sitting in chairs, crew members wear ties around their legs to hold themselves in place. Magnets hold forks, knives and spoons on the trays.

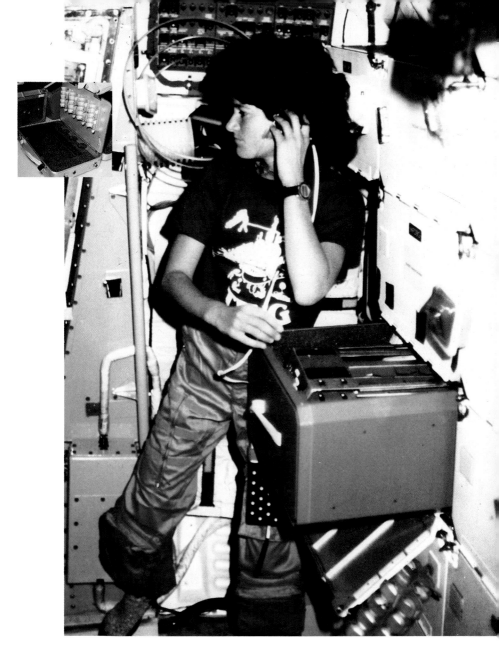

Mission specialist Sally K. Ride listens to ground controllers from the mid-deck of the space shuttle Challenger. The mid-deck is also where the crew members eat, sleep and relax. Inset: A food warmer designed for use on the shuttle heats cocoa, coffee and tea. Springs hold the beverage packets in place.

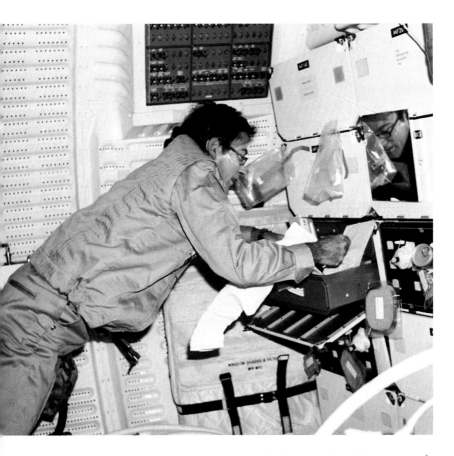

Astronaut John Young shaves in the mid-deck area on the STS-1 mission of Columbia.

Before leaving the Kennedy Space Center, the crew gets a menu for each day of the trip. Breakfast might include orange drink, peaches, scrambled eggs, sausage, cocoa and a sweet roll. For lunch the crew might dine on mushroom soup, ham-and-cheese sandwiches, stewed tomatoes, a banana and cookies. Dinner might provide shrimp cocktail, steak, broccoli with cheese, strawberries, pudding and coffee.

Crew members take turns being chef for the day. The day's chef adds water to food containers for each crew member. The food is then heated in an oven and put on the food trays. The moisture in the food makes it stick to the side of the container. Moisture also holds it on a fork or spoon, so astronauts can use utensils to eat. Air currents carry loose crumbs into a filter system.

Other food is served in cans and foil pouches. Most of the food is dried or canned to preserve it. Cookies, nuts and some other foods do not have to be preserved.

For those who do not like the day's meal, there are snacks in the pantry. It takes about five minutes plus heating time to prepare a meal for four. Menus are repeated every six days. In the future, scientists hope to be able to grow gardens in space to supply food to space station crews.

Keeping Clean

Keeping the spacecraft clean is an important chore. In such a small area, germs are likely to spread quickly. All members of the crew clean the food and dining areas, the toilet and the sleeping areas. With no washing machine on board, the astronauts seal dirty clothes in plastic bags. They change pants twice a week, socks and underwear every day. They have one shirt for every three days of the trip.

Garbage, trash and dirty food containers are stored in plastic bags. Crew members use wet wipes to clean their trays and utensils. There are no dirty dishes to clean!

The shuttle's toilet looks almost like one on Earth. Air sucks wastes into the tank. Then water is removed from the wastes, which are then sealed in plastic bags. Scientists study some of the wastes to see how the body reacts in space.

There is no room for a shower on the shuttle. The crew members wash themselves with sponges. When it is bath time, each astronaut shoots hot water onto a sponge with a squirt gun. After washing, the astronauts squeeze their sponges dry. The dirty water flows into a waste storage tank.

Shaving raises other problems. Astronauts use shaving cream and a safety razor and wipe away the cut hairs with a towel. If the tiny hairs got loose they could damage equipment.

TRAGEDY ABOARD THE CHALLENGER

B y the beginning of 1986 NASA's four shuttles had flown 24 successful missions. Between them they had orbited the Earth more than 2,400 times. They had traveled 57 million miles, the equivalent of more than 118 round trips to the Moon.

The *Challenger* had flown nine successful missions, more than any other shuttle. It had orbited Earth 987 times.

The space shuttle Challenger *explodes shortly after launch on January 28, 1986. Inset: New Hampshire teacher S. Christa McAuliffe was selected to be the first teacher in space. She died with the rest of the crew in the* Challenger *explosion.*

The *Challenger* had many feats to its credit. It had been the first shuttle to launch and land at night. Its crew had been first to capture and repair a satellite in space. Now it was getting ready to carry the first private citizen into space.

NASA chose S. Christa McAuliffe, a teacher in New Hampshire, to fly aboard the *Challenger*. Once in space she would teach a lesson that would be broadcast to students all over the world. Her crew members were Francis R. "Dick" Scobee, Michael J. Smith, Ellison S. Onizuka, Ronald E. McNair, Gregory B. Jarvis and Judith A. Resnik.

On January 28, 1986, at 11:38 A.M., Mission 51-L took off from Launchpad 39B at the Kennedy Space Center. The day was bright and cold. Earlier the temperature had dropped below freezing. Shortly before lift-off the main engines ignited. A few seconds later the solid rocket boosters fired, and the *Challenger* lifted off from the launchpad. Thirty-five seconds into the flight the main engines were throttled back to ease the strain on the shuttle. Seventeen seconds more and the engines opened up to send the *Challenger* into space. It was moving at 1,977 mph.

At 73 seconds after lift-off a flame burst out of one of the solid rocket boosters and shot upward. Then the orbiter and the external tank became a ball of fire. The solid rocket boosters, trailing white smoke, veered away from the orbiter. In a mass of white smoke the orbiter spun wildly, then broke apart. All seven crew members were killed.

The *Challenger* disaster almost killed the shuttle program too. For four months a panel of experts studied the *Challenger* explosion. No other flights lifted off in 1986. None flew in 1987.

The accident was blamed on a rubber seal that was

supposed to prevent hot gases from leaking through the joint in the solid rocket motor. Called an O-ring because of its shape, the seal apparently contracted in the cold. That allowed hot gases to leak out and burn a hole in the external tank. The liquid hydrogen in the tank caught fire and exploded.

After the disaster, NASA overhauled the entire shuttle program. More than 200 changes were made in the systems. The main engines, brakes, landing gear and tiles were improved. A valve allowed crews to unhook the tank quickly from the orbiter. Parachutes were designed to carry the crew to safety in a crisis. Following the advice of experts, NASA changed the way the program was run.

After 32 months the shuttle program was back in business. *Discovery* lifted off from Launchpad 39B on September 29, 1988. It carried the satellite in its payload that the *Challenger* was to have delivered to space. Before landing, the crew of the *Discovery* paid a tribute to the *Challenger* crew.

SCUTTLE THE SHUTTLE?

B y the end of 1991 the shuttle had made 44 successful flights in ten years. That is almost twice as many as in the Mercury, Gemini and Apollo programs combined.

The shuttle has carried satellites into space and repaired others while in orbit. Satellites installed by the shuttle crew allow people all over the world to communicate with each other. Other satellites send back information on the weather, pollution and energy. Data from satellites help in making maps and improving farming and fishing.

Students have sent up experiments as well. One showed that honeybees could build a honeycomb in space. The honeycomb was crooked at first, but the bees straightened it out by the end of the trip.

In 1988 NASA launched the second of two satellites that keep track of spacecraft. The Tracking and Data Relay Satellite system orbits over Earth's equator. It can track 24 orbiting spacecraft at the same time. The system replaces about half of NASA's ground tracking stations. The old system kept track of spacecraft only about 15 percent of the time. With the new system NASA is in touch with spacecraft 85 to 95 percent of the time.

Working in Spacelab, researchers make drugs they cannot make on Earth. Others grow crystals as much as 1,000 times larger than those grown on Earth. The crystals are used to run modern electronic devices. In space, experts can mix metals to make new materials not found on Earth. Glass for lenses is much clearer when made in space.

In April 1990 the shuttle launched the *Hubble* space telescope into space. The telescope sent back pictures much farther away in the galaxy than had ever been seen before. But because of a faulty mirror, the telescope is hard to focus. A shuttle crew may have to repair it.

The shuttle has also launched space probes, craft that shoot into space and explore unknown regions. On October 18, 1989, the shuttle sent *Galileo* on its way to Jupiter. Unfortunately this probe's main antenna did not open properly. Scientists are trying to fix it from Earth, using radio waves. If all goes well the probe may be the first to orbit the outer planets and sample the gases around them.

Despite the shuttle's successes, concerns about danger,

Astronauts F. Story Musgrave (left) and Donald H. Peterson float in the cargo bay of the space shuttle Challenger *during its first mission in 1983. The first Tracking and Data Relay Satellite was released into space during the mission.*

Space shuttle Discovery roars into space from its launchpad at the Kennedy Space Center on mission STS-29. The shuttle, launched March 13, 1989, carried a Tracking and Data Relay Satellite into orbit.

cost and delay may end the program. From the start the shuttle program has been plagued by problems. It was supposed to cost $5.15 billion to develop, but ended up costing $9.9 billion.

The first launch was delayed two and a half years while builders worked on design problems. Most of the flights have been delayed for hours or days because of faulty equipment. The system is so complex that a problem in any one of thousands of parts can lead to failure.

Weather is also a problem. The shuttle cannot launch in clouds or fog. The pilot must be able to see the runway if an emergency landing has to be made. High winds and bad weather have delayed both launches and landings. The delays add to the cost of each flight.

According to NASA the delays are proof that the shuttle's safety systems work. Critics of the space program have blamed the delays on a badly designed system. They have said the shuttle is not safe.

Some experts say it would be cheaper and safer to use unpiloted rockets to send cargo to space. It now costs from $3,000 to $10,000 a pound to launch a payload aboard the shuttle. A new unpiloted rocket being designed may lower the cost to $300 a pound. The new rocket would not be reused.

Under one plan no new shuttles would be built. The four space shuttles already built would continue to be used.

Despite its drawbacks, the shuttle has taken us farther into space than ever before. It has carried one million pounds of cargo into orbit and has traveled the distance from Earth to the Sun. It has orbited Earth 4,000 times.

The shuttle may someday serve as a model for a national space plane that can take off from a runway. And it may play a key role in building the *Freedom* **space station**, which may lead us to Mars.

The shuttle and space programs before it have given us a bigger view of space. When the first shuttle lifted off in 1981, the pilot Robert L. Crippen's pulse shot up to 135. It was normally around 60. Looking into space he shouted, "Man, what a feeling, what a view!"

Someday we too may feel the excitement of a ride in space.

GLOSSARY

air lock A sealed room leading from the shuttle's cabin to the payload bay and to space. The sealed air lock keeps the cabin's air and pressure from escaping when the hatch is open.

astronaut A space explorer.

Challenger The second U.S. space shuttle. It exploded after lift-off on January 28, 1986, killing all seven crew members aboard.

Columbia The first U.S. space shuttle.

commander The astronaut in charge of a mission.

external tank The aluminum tank that holds liquid hydrogen and liquid oxygen to fuel the shuttle's main engines.

flight deck The upper level of the cabin, where the pilot and commander operate the shuttle.

Freedom **space station** A permanent laboratory planned to be built in space by the year 2000 by the United States, Canada, Japan and the 14 countries of the European Space Agency.

gravity The force that pulls us toward Earth.

KC-135 jet The "vomit comet," used to produce the feeling of weightlessness found in space.

mid-deck The lower level of the cabin, where the crew lives during a shuttle flight.

mission specialist An astronaut who plans activities on the shuttle and keeps things running smoothly, and is in charge of the equipment needed for payloads and experiments.

National Aeronautics and Space Administration (NASA)
The government agency in charge of the U.S. space program.

orbit To revolve around another body in space.

orbiter The main body of the space shuttle.

oxidizer Material used to make fuel burn. Oxygen serves as an oxidizer for the liquid hydrogen in the shuttle's external tank.

payload The cargo, or load, carried by a spacecraft.

payload bay The area to the rear of the shuttle where the cargo is stored.

payload specialist The crew member, not an astronaut, in charge of the payload and chosen by the company that owns the payload. He or she must be approved by NASA.

pilot The second in command on a shuttle flight. He or she helps the commander run the shuttle.

robot arm An automated, metal arm used to load and unload the shuttle's cargo in space.

satellite A small body that orbits, or circles, a larger body in space.

shuttle The first reusable U.S. spacecraft.

simulator A copy of the inside of the shuttle, used to practice for space flight.

solid rocket boosters The two rockets on either side of the shuttle, which boost the spacecraft into space. The main engines also provide power for lift-off.

thrust The forward push of a rocket as gases are forced out the rocket's tail.

SUGGESTED READING

Barrett, N. S. *Space Shuttle*. New York: Franklin Watts, 1985.

Berger, Melvin. *Space Shots, Shuttles and Satellites*. New York: Putnam, 1983.

Billings, Charlene W. *Christa McAuliffe: Pioneer Space Teacher*. New York: Enslow Publishers, Inc., 1986.

——————————. *Space Station: Bold New Step Beyond Earth*. New York: Dodd, Mead, 1986.

Dwiggins, Don. *Flying the Space Shuttles*. New York: Dodd, Mead, 1985.

Embury, Barbara, and Thomas D. Crouch. *The Dream Is Alive*. New York: Harper & Row, 1990.

Fichter, George S. *The Space Shuttle*. New York: Franklin Watts, 1981.

Fox, Mary Virginia. *Women Astronauts: Aboard the Shuttle*. New York: J. Messner, 1984.

Fradin, Dennis B. *Spacelab*. Chicago: Children's Press, 1984.

Friskey, Margaret. *Space Shuttles*. Chicago: Children's Press, 1982.

Haskins, Jim, and Kathleen Benson. *Space Challenger: The Story of Guion Bluford*. Minneapolis: Carolrhoda Books, 1984.

Hawkes, Nigel. *Space Shuttle*. New York: Gloucester Press, 1983.

Herda, D. J. *Communications Satellites*. New York: Franklin Watts, 1988.

Kohn, Bernice. *Communications Satellites: Message Centers in Space*. New York: Four Winds Press, 1975.

Lampton, Christopher. *The Space Telescope*. New York: Franklin Watts, 1987.

McCarter, James. *The Space Shuttle Disaster*. New York: Bookwright Press, 1988.

Naden, Corinne. *Ronald McNair, Astronaut*. New York: Chelsea House Publishers, 1991.

Ride, Sally, and Susan Okie. *To Space and Back*. New York: Lothrop, Lee & Shepard, 1986.

Weiss, Malcolm E. *Far Out Factories: Manufacturing in Space*. New York: Lodestar Books, 1984.

INDEX